THE EUGÉNIE ROCHEROLLE SERIES

Intermediate Piano Solo

AUDIO ACCESS INCLUDED

Classic Jazz Standards

10 Favorites Arranged by Eugénie Rocherolle

PLAYBACK+

Speed • Pitch • Balance • Loop

To access audio visit:
www.halleonard.com/mylibrary

Enter Code
7204-6035-9625-2620

ISBN: 978-1-4234-2965-4

HAL•LEONARD®
CORPORATION
7777 W. BLUEMOUND RD. P.O. BOX 13819 MILWAUKEE, WI 53213

Visit Hal Leonard Online at
www.halleonard.com

BLUE SKIES
from BETSY

Words and Music by IRVING BERLIN
Arranged by Eugénie Rocherolle

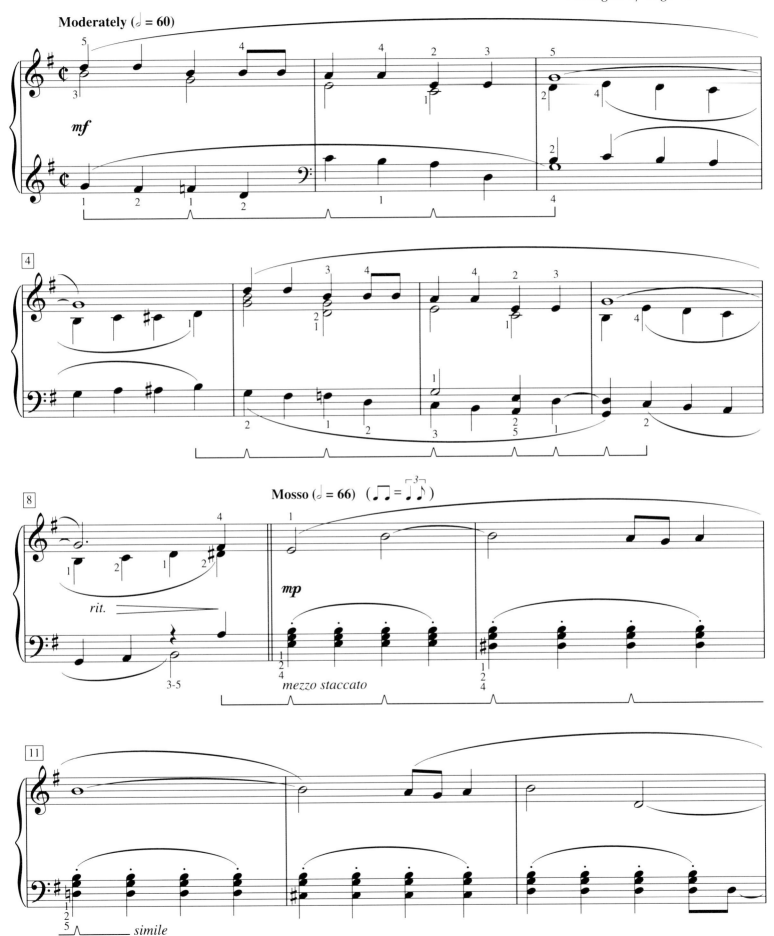

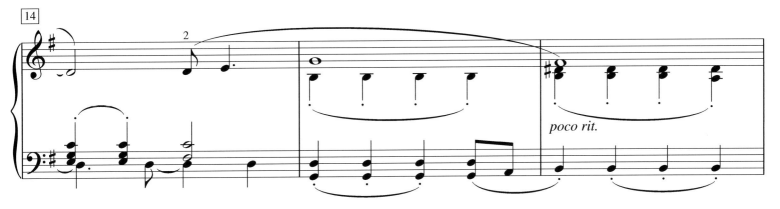

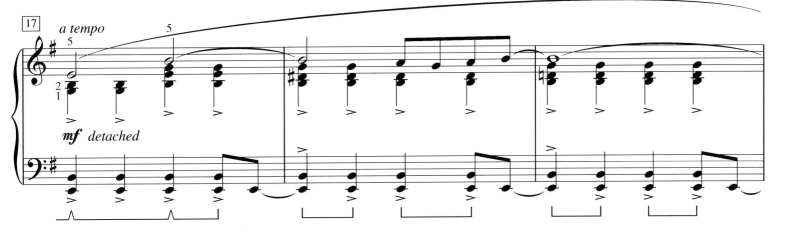

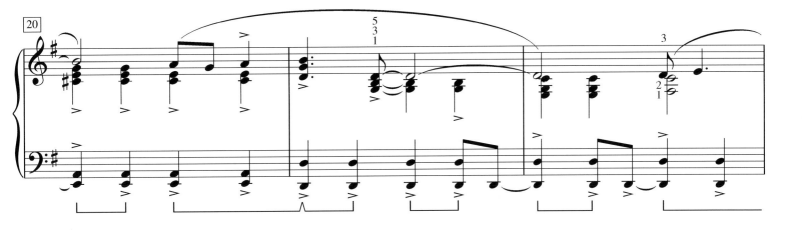

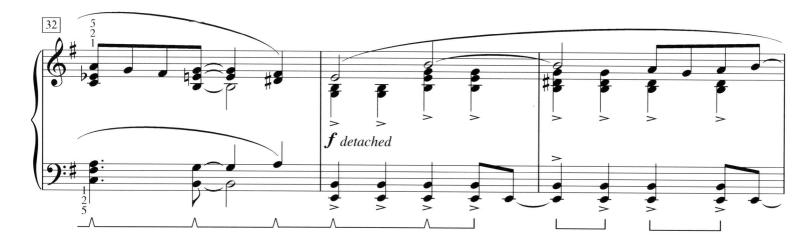

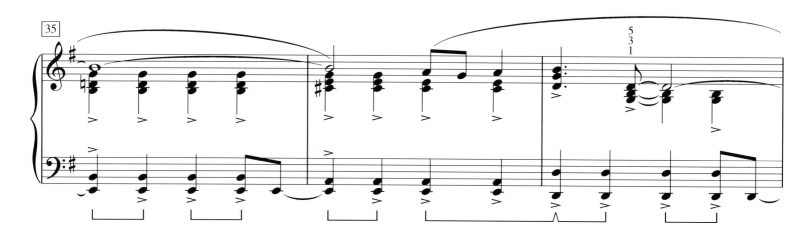

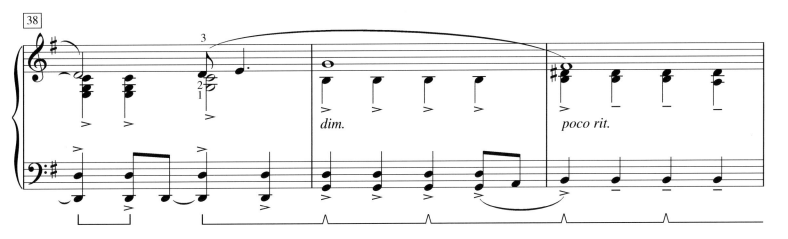

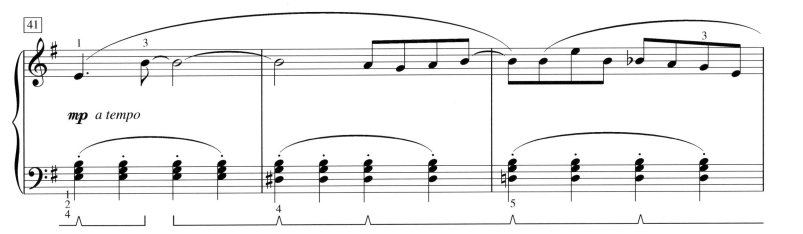

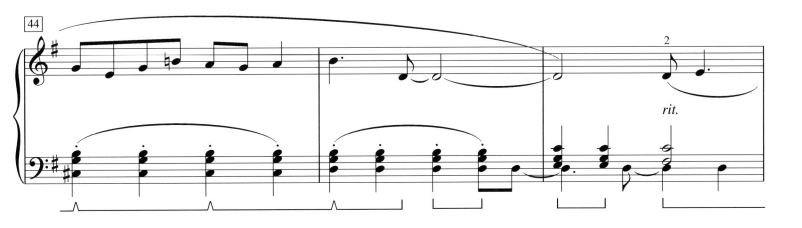

(I Love You)
FOR SENTIMENTAL REASONS

Words by DEEK WATSON
Music by WILLIAM BEST
Arranged by Eugénie Rocherolle

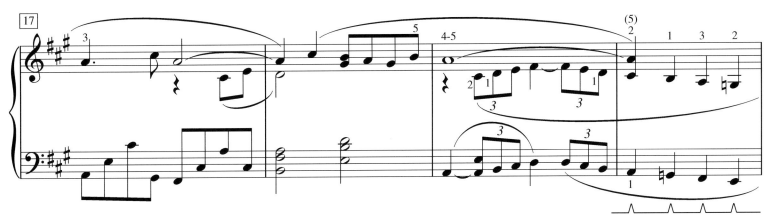

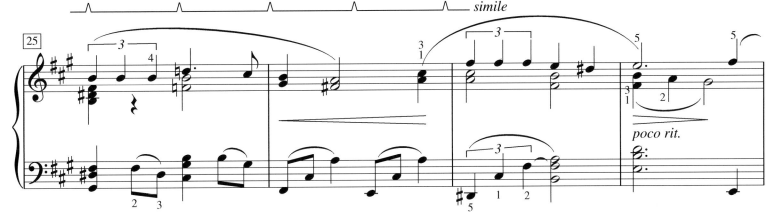

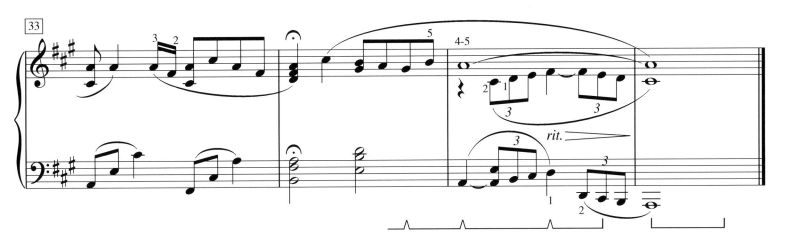

GEORGIA ON MY MIND

Words by STUART GORRELL
Music by HOAGY CARMICHAEL
Arranged by Eugénie Rocherolle

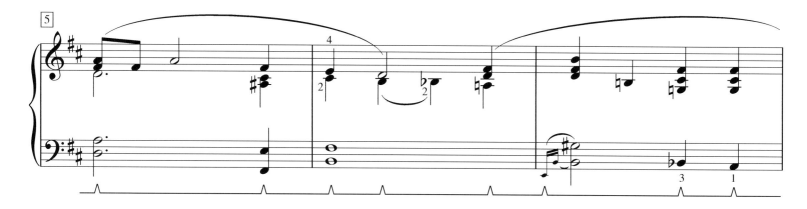

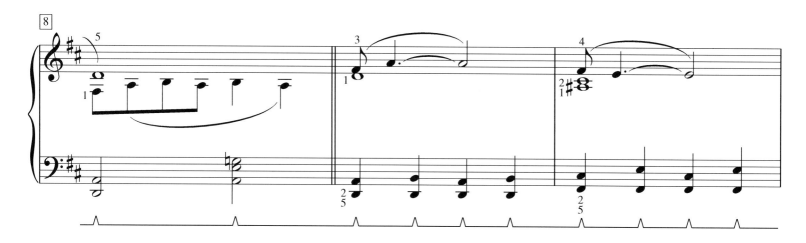

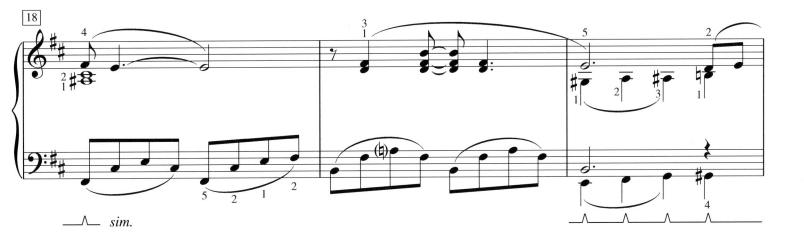

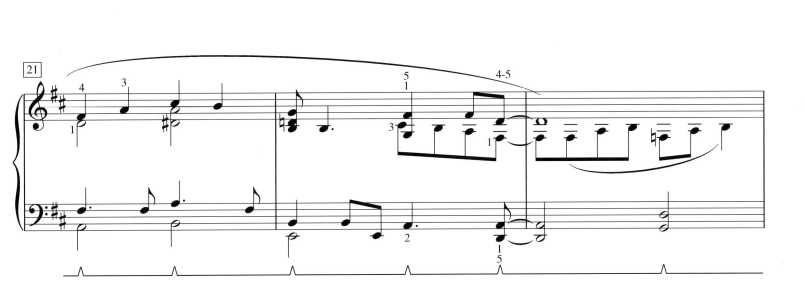

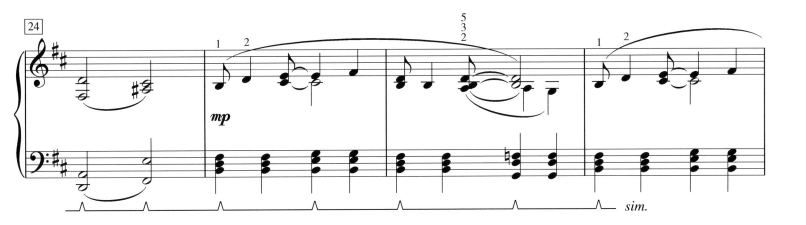

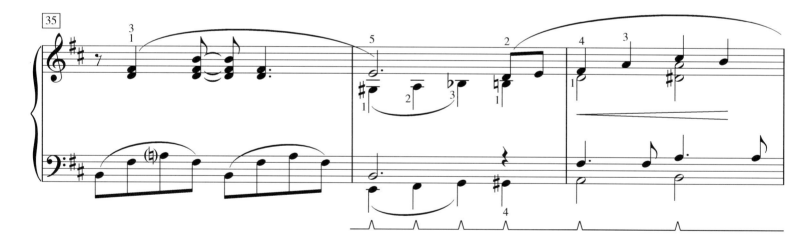

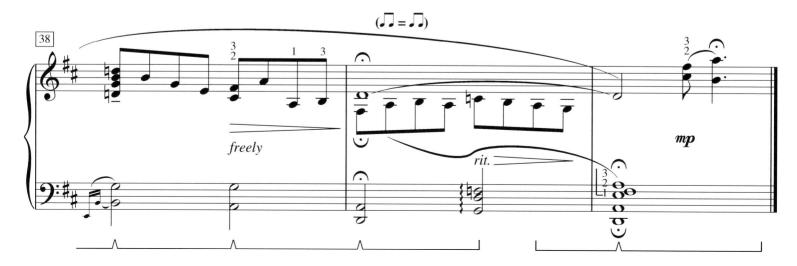

I'VE GOT THE WORLD ON A STRING

Lyric by TED KOEHLER
Music by HAROLD ARLEN
Arranged by Eugénie Rocherolle

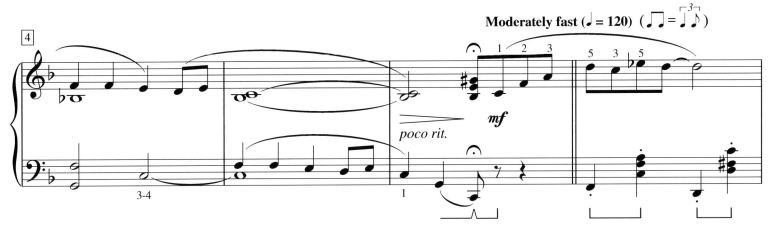

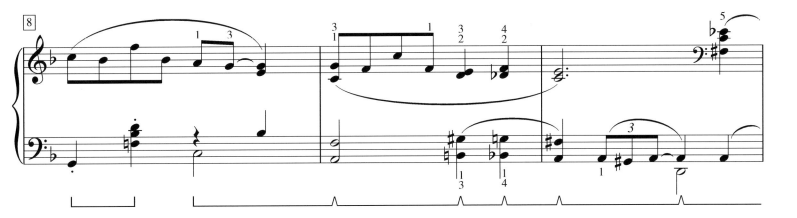

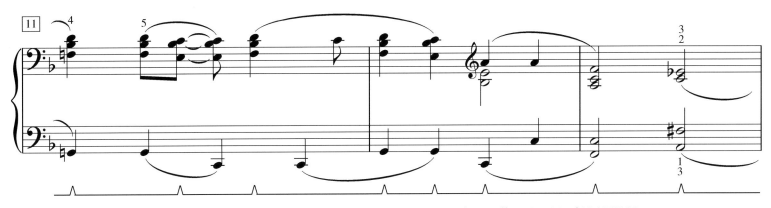

12

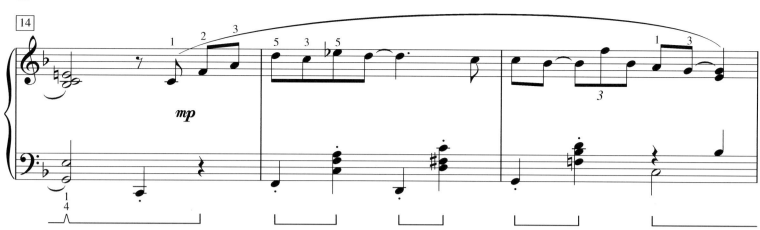

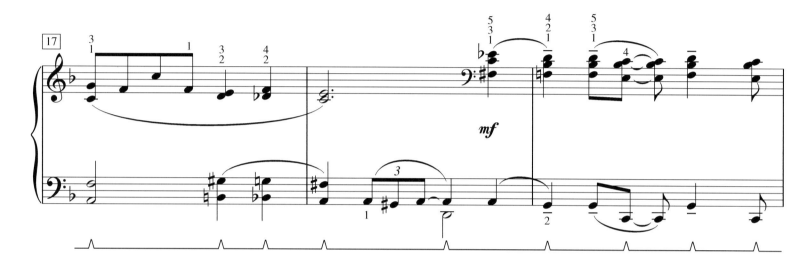

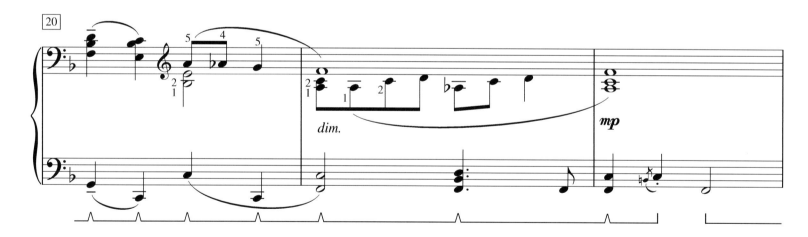

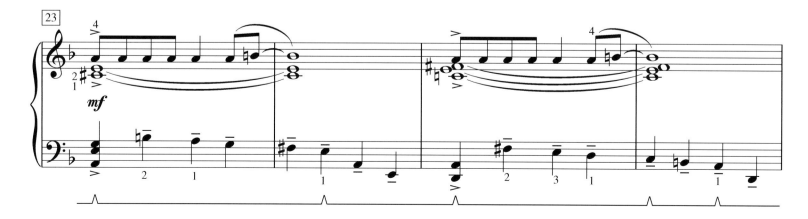

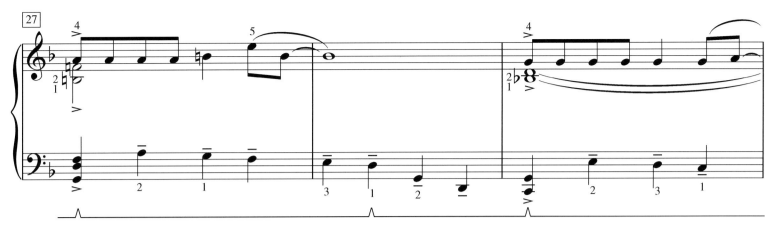

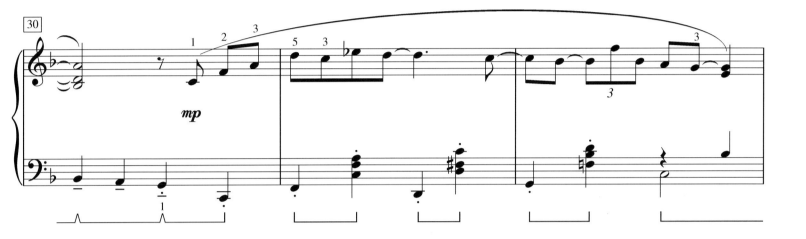

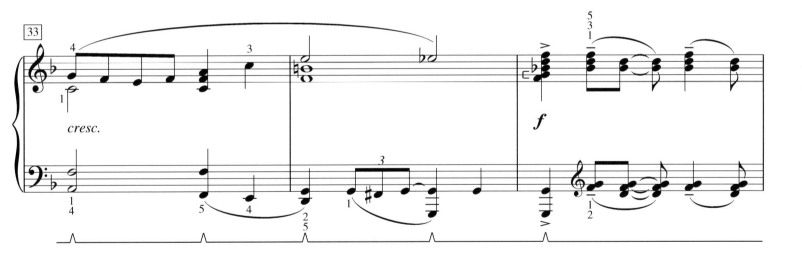

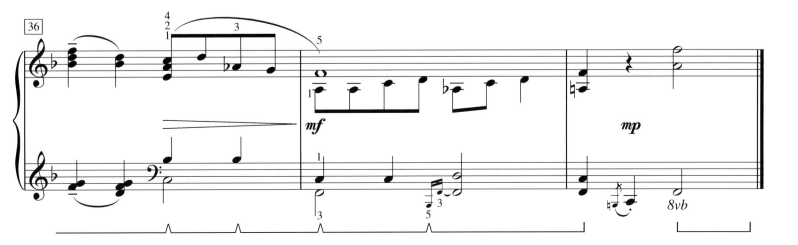

LAZY RIVER

Words and Music by HOAGY CARMICHAEL
and SIDNEY ARODIN
Arranged by Eugénie Rocherolle

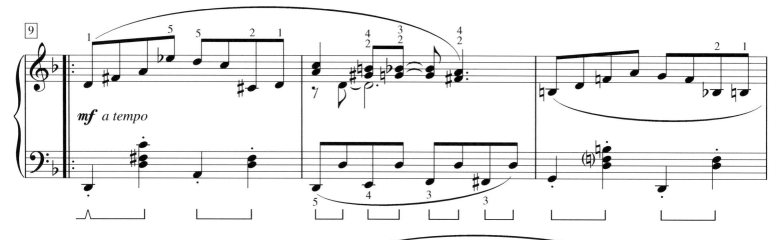

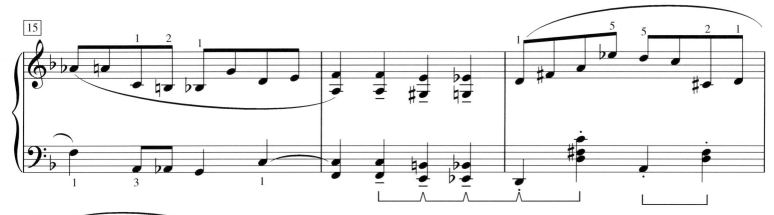

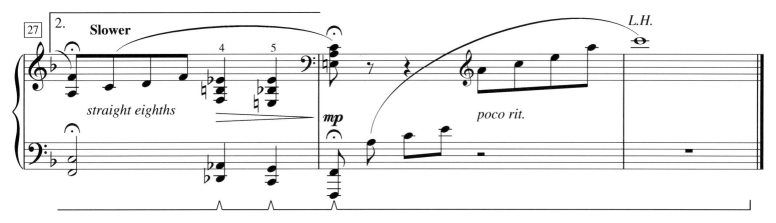

ISN'T IT ROMANTIC?
from the Paramount Picture LOVE ME TONIGHT

Words by LORENZ HART
Music by RICHARD RODGERS
Arranged by Eugénie Rocherolle

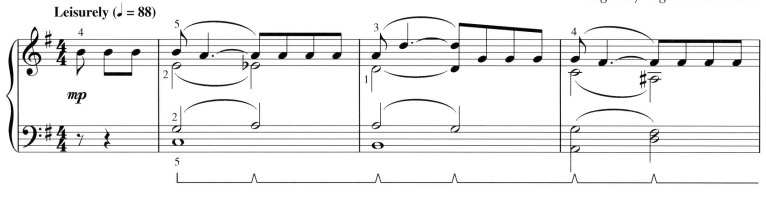

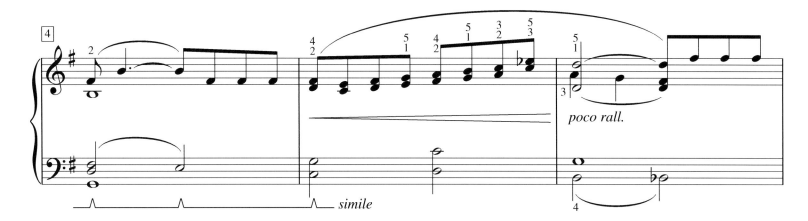

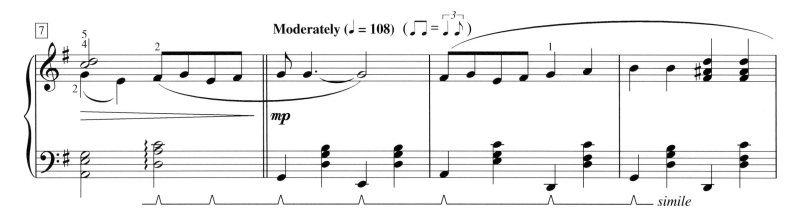

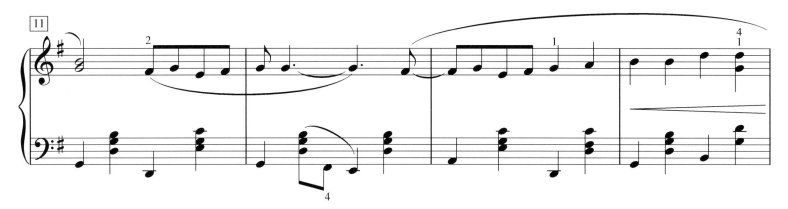

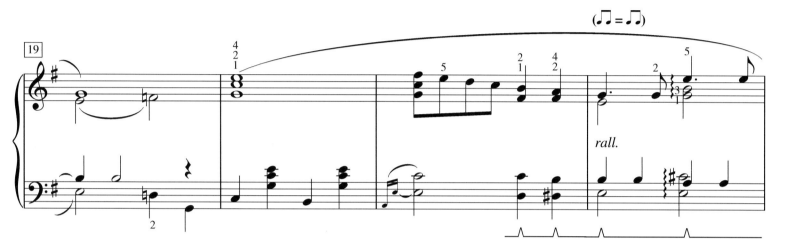

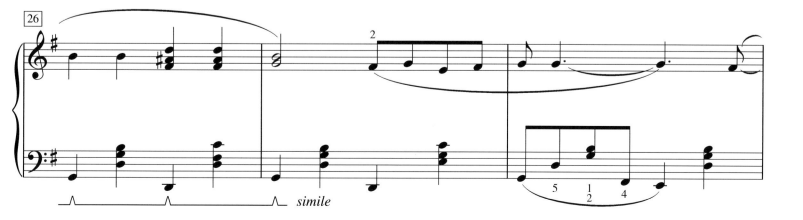

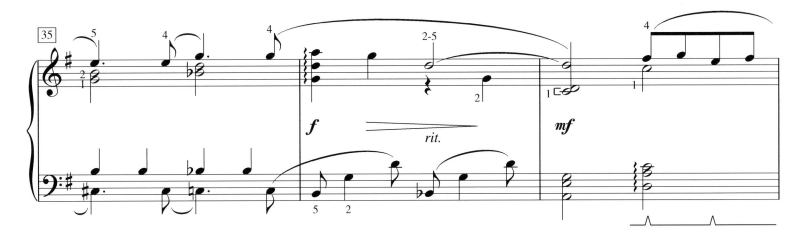

THE NEARNESS OF YOU
from the Paramount Picture ROMANCE IN THE DARK

Words by NED WASHINGTON
Music by HOAGY CARMICHAEL
Arranged by Eugénie Rocherolle

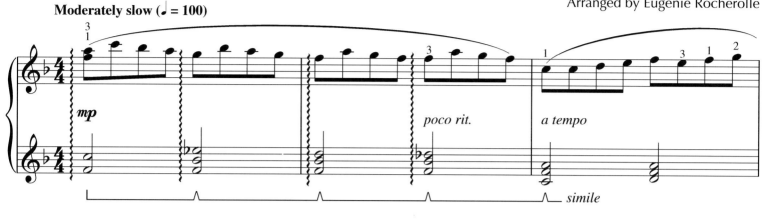

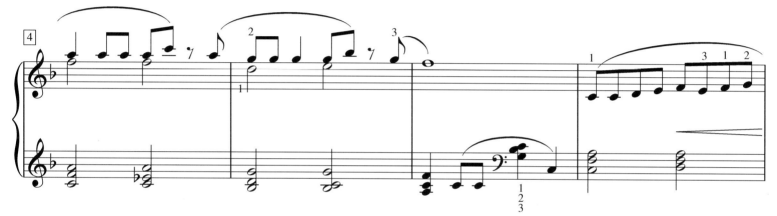

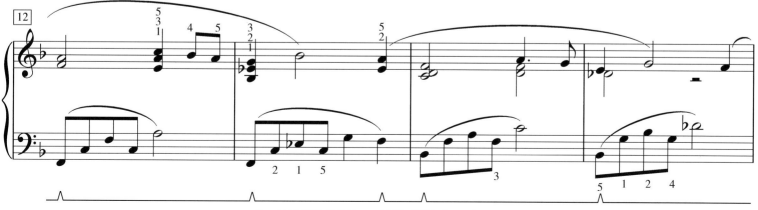

20

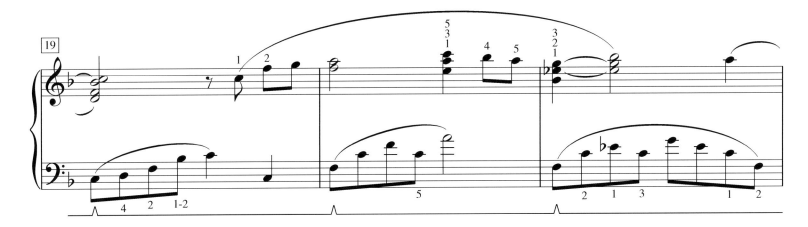

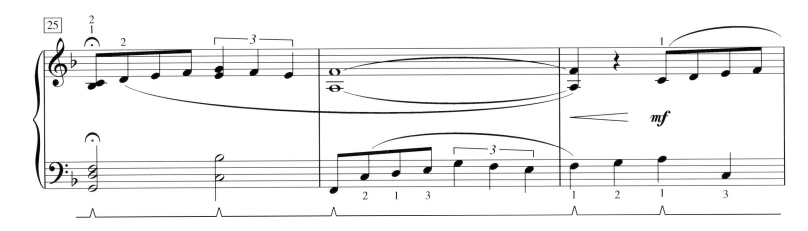

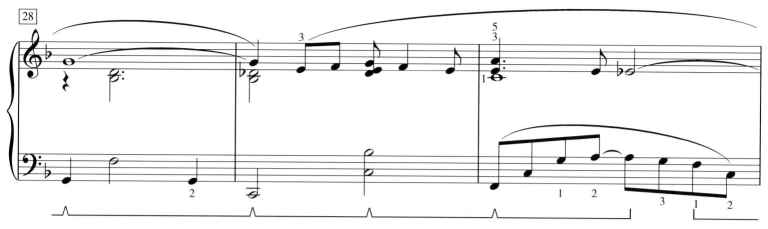

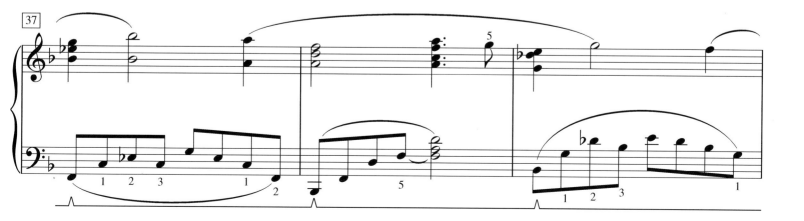

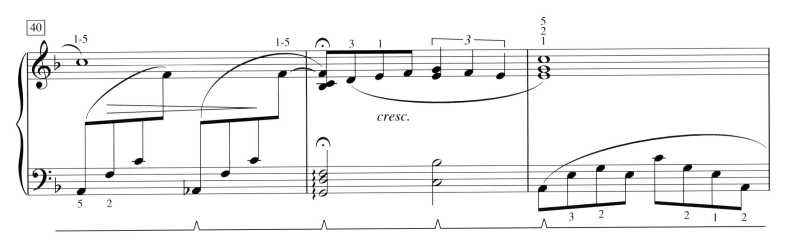

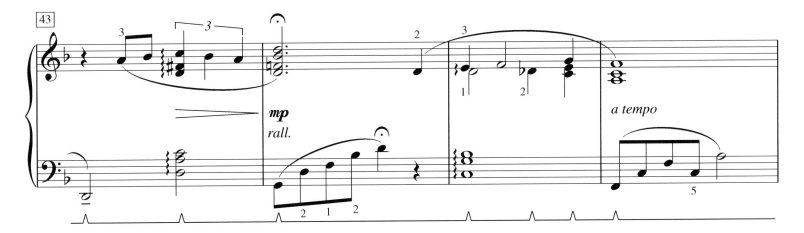

ON THE SUNNY SIDE OF THE STREET

Lyric by DOROTHY FIELDS
Music by JIMMY McHUGH
Arranged by Eugénie Rocherolle

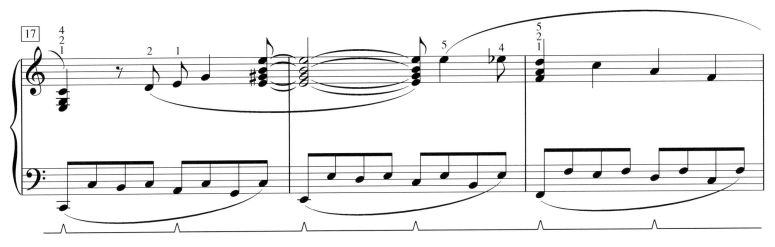

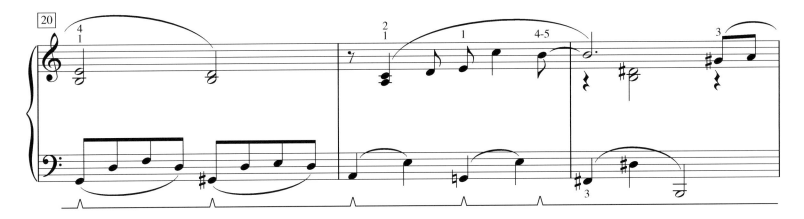

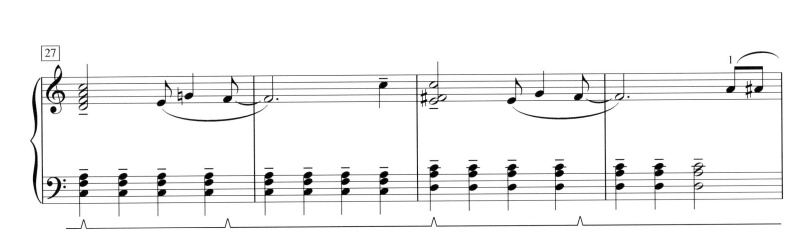

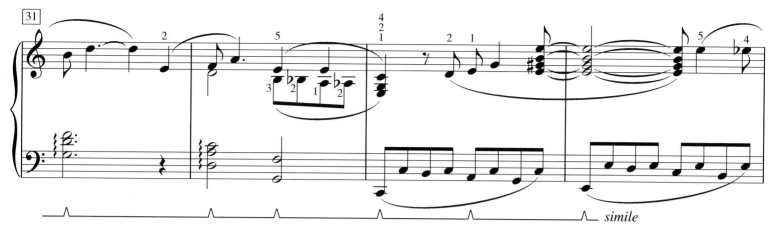

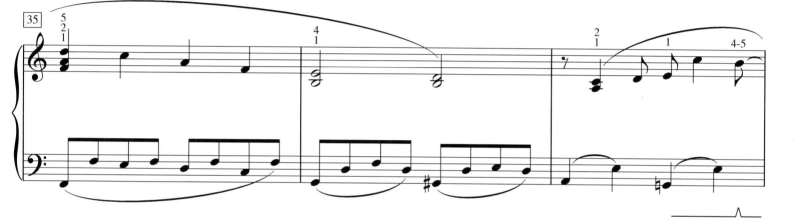

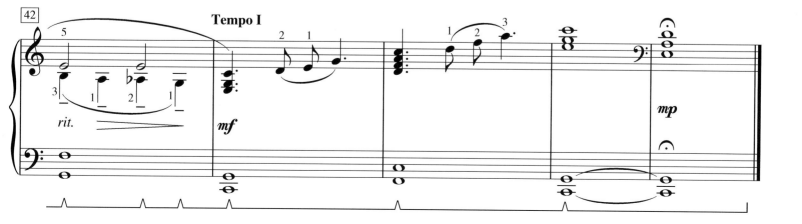

STARDUST

Words by MITCHELL PARISH
Music by HOAGY CARMICHAEL
Arranged by Eugénie Rocherolle

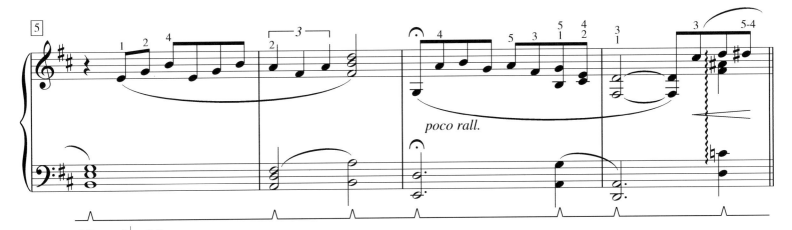

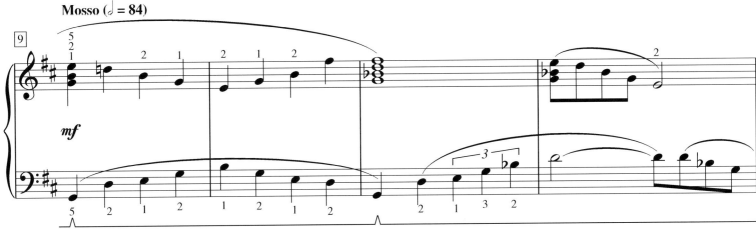

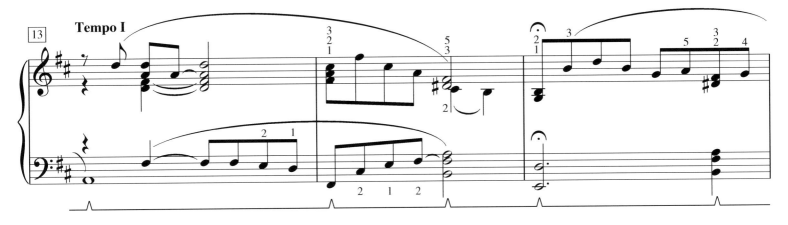

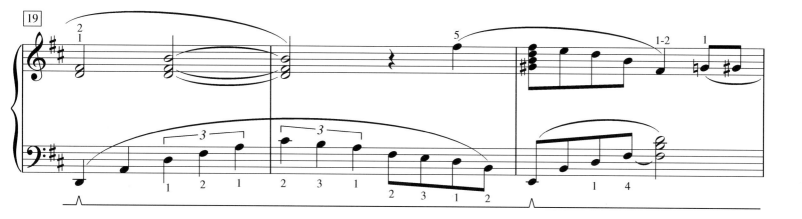

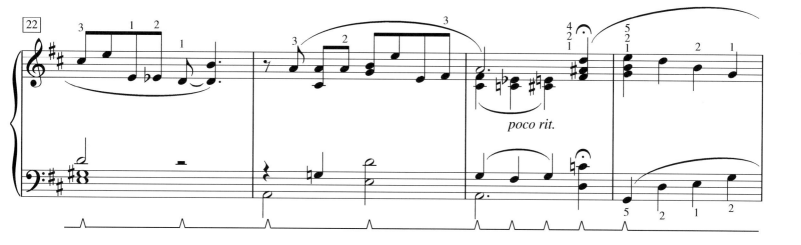

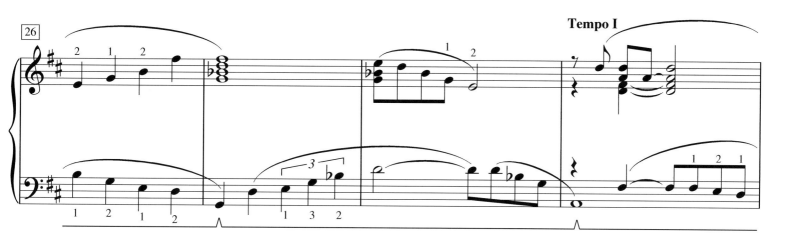

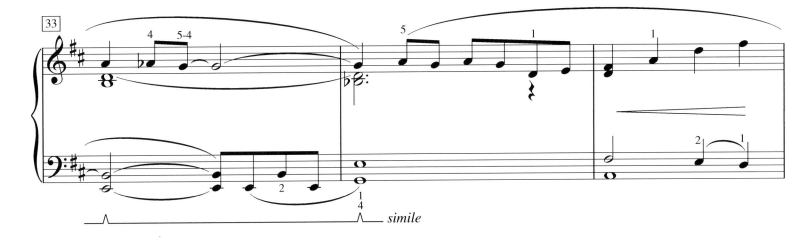

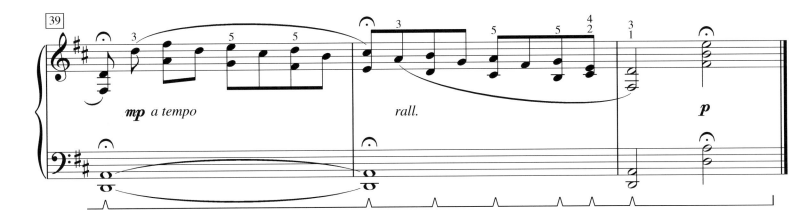

STORMY WEATHER
(Keeps Rainin' All the Time)

Lyric by TED KOEHLER
Music by HAROLD ARLEN
Arranged by Eugénie Rocherolle

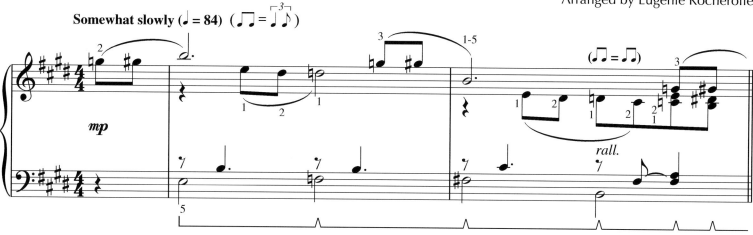

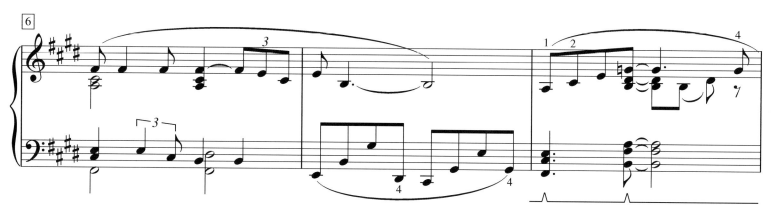

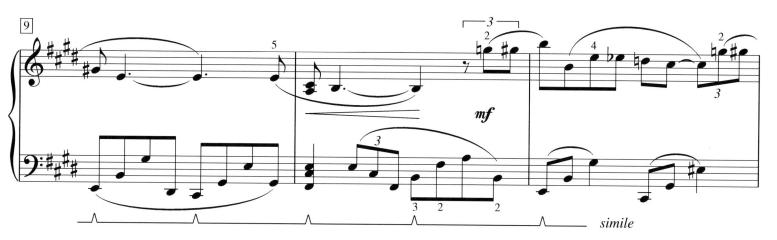

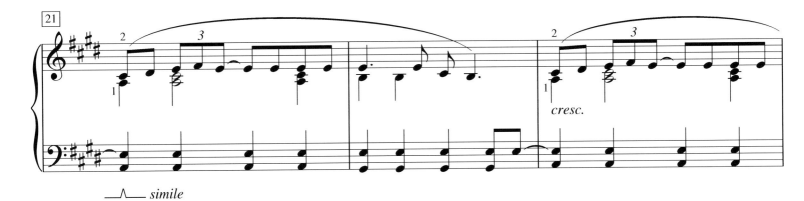

cresc.

simile

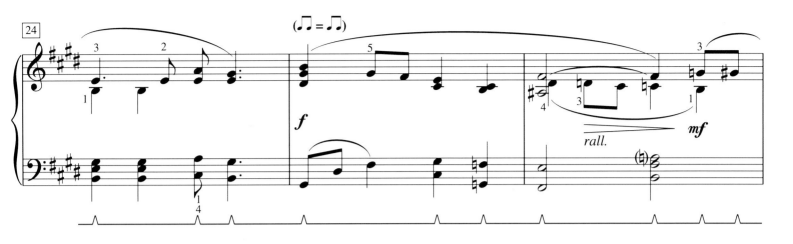

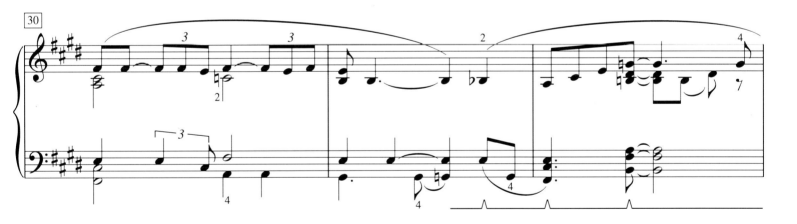